# Rebel
# Artists

## Contents

Written by Thomas Bloor

# Collins

# 1 Introduction

A long, long time ago, somewhere in the darkened recesses of a cave, an unknown person decided to make some marks on a rough stone wall. They might have used the burnt end of a stick or perhaps some richly-coloured clay, applied with their fingers. We'll never know for certain what the first-ever cave paintings looked like, or who made them, or why they did so. But whatever their reasons, they'd found a way to show how they thought, or how they felt, about life and the world around them.

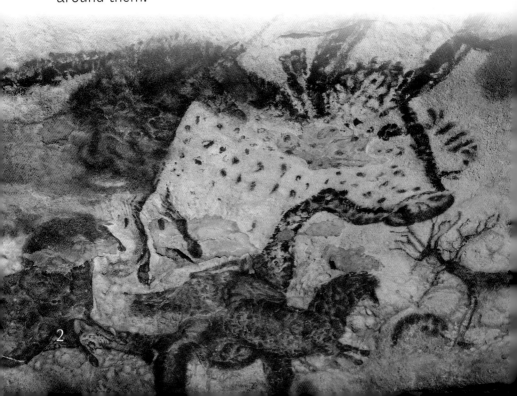

What would other people have made of it, when they understood what this first-ever artist had done? Would they have been impressed? Suspicious? Frightened? Again, we will never know. But ever since then, artists of all kinds, from all across the world, have been coming up with new ways of seeing and making sense of their world. They've found new methods for creating art, in ways that often challenge how things were done before, and define how they'll be done in the future. They are revolutionaries and mould-breakers. They are rebel artists.

# 2 Giuseppe Arcimboldo (1527-93)

Arcimboldo was born in Milan, in what is now Italy, in 1527. Not much is known about his life. In those days, the kings and queens of Europe would employ artists to paint their portraits and to decorate their palaces and castles. Arcimboldo was one of these court painters. He painted in the traditional style favoured by the rulers of Europe at the time.

Self portrait (1570)

This was how Arcimboldo made his living. There was nothing remarkable about most of his work. Nowadays, that side of his art has been largely forgotten.

Portrait of Archduchess Anna of Austria by Arcimboldo (1563)

4

But it was not the only art he produced. Arcimboldo was also known for a very unusual type of portrait and not the sort of thing you normally saw hanging on the walls of a grand palace.

Can you imagine a man made of fish? It seems impossible, doesn't it? Not to Arcimboldo. He could paint a face made from anything – fruit, vegetables, even books. Arcimboldo would paint each object in great detail, as in a **still-life painting**, but he'd show them piled up and stuck together in such a way as to create a human face.

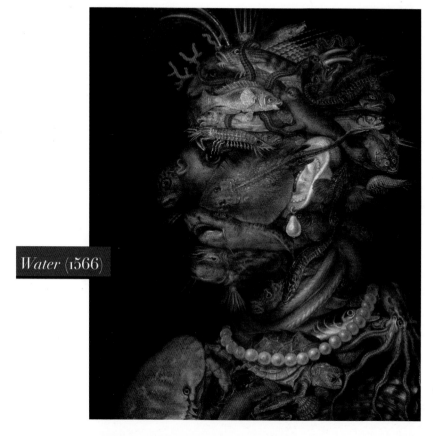

Water (1566)

*Four Seasons in One Head* (1590)

Why did Arcimboldo paint portraits like this? Was it a way of criticising or poking fun at his royal subjects? To some, a painting of a man as half-human, half-vegetable might look monstrous, like something from a nightmare. And yet these were portraits of real people. Arcimboldo might have been able to portray himself as a monster – *Four Seasons in One Head* is said to be a self-portrait – but it's unlikely he would have got away with depicting his powerful masters this way, not unless the kings and noblemen were in on the joke.

*Reversible Head with Basket of Fruit* (1590)

It's now believed the paintings were seen as amusing. They were something new, something different, and important people seemed to like them. King Augustus of Saxony, for instance, who visited Vienna in 1570, saw one of Arcimboldo's works and paid for a copy to be painted to take home with him.

Nevertheless, after his death in 1593, Arcimboldo's work was quickly forgotten. It wasn't until the early 20th century, when a group of artists called the Surrealists became interested in making art from the world of dreams and nightmares, that Arcimboldo's strange portraits became popular once more.

*The Librarian* (1566)

# 3 Hokusai
## (1760-1849)

More than a hundred and fifty years later, and thousands of kilometres away, a six-year-old boy was beginning to practise the skills that would one day make him famous. His name was Hokusai, and he was learning to be an artist.

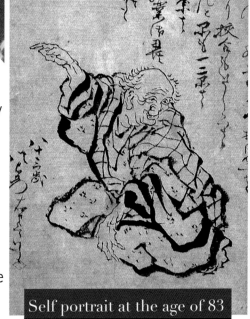

Self portrait at the age of 83

Hokusai was born in the city of Edo (now Tokyo) in Japan. He's known to have used at least thirty different names throughout his life, changing names whenever he found a new way to make art. It was not that unusual for artists to do this in Japan at the time, but Hokusai seems to have changed his name more times than most. This was not the only rebellious thing he would do.

At that time, it was traditional to study at the school of one master artist. Students were expected to stick rigidly to the artistic style of their school. Hokusai, however, studied under more than one master at a time. He also challenged the rules about the sort of subjects artists could depict. Hokusai drew and painted anything he wanted, including landscapes, plants and animals. Until then, the only subject seen as suitable had been people.

*The Great Wave off Kanagawa* (1833)

And yet Hokusai became a successful and well-known artist in his day, producing paintings, illustrations, prints and educational books. He called these books "manga".

*Hokusai Manga* (early 19th century)

Nowadays, the word manga is used to describe a kind of Japanese comic-book art. But Hokusai's manga were a series of books containing thousands of drawings of every subject you could think of, intended to help others learn how to draw anything they wanted.

contemporary print of Hokusai painting
a giant portrait in 1817

One reason for Hokusai's success was that he was very good at self-publicity. He once gave an outdoor demonstration of his skill by making a gigantic portrait, said to be 200 square metres in size. A crowd watched him using a broom for a brush, dipped into buckets full of ink. The result was just as good as when he used more traditional-sized paintbrushes.

*Fine Wind, Clear Morning* (1833)

Hokusai also never stopped wanting to learn about art, to find new ways to work. On his deathbed, aged 88, he said, "Just another five more years, then I could become a real painter."

Mary Cassatt was born in North America, five years before Hokusai's death. She would grow up to be part of the European art movement known as the Impressionists.

Self portrait (1880)

The Impressionists were a group of artists who rebelled against the old style of painting. In Europe at the time, artists almost always worked on their paintings in a **studio**. They often spent months working on each **canvas**. Scenes from old myths and legends were popular, with carefully-posed figures and detailed backgrounds.

*The Lady of Shalott* (1862) by Walter Crane, an example of the classic style of painting in Mary Cassatt's time

The Impressionists, on the other hand, took their painting equipment out of the studio. They worked quickly, often finishing a painting in less than an hour. They wanted to capture an "impression" of the light, wherever they were, exactly as they saw it, then and there.

Sketch *Mother Looking Down at Thomas* (1915)

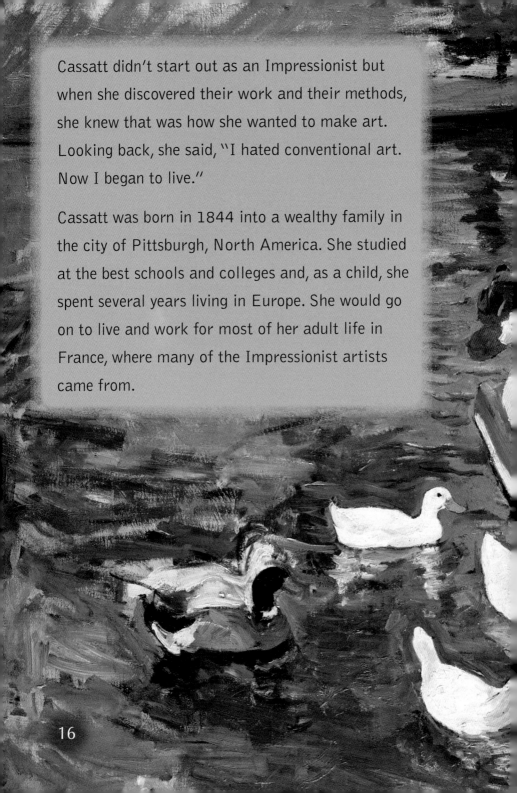

Cassatt didn't start out as an Impressionist but when she discovered their work and their methods, she knew that was how she wanted to make art. Looking back, she said, "I hated conventional art. Now I began to live."

Cassatt was born in 1844 into a wealthy family in the city of Pittsburgh, North America. She studied at the best schools and colleges and, as a child, she spent several years living in Europe. She would go on to live and work for most of her adult life in France, where many of the Impressionist artists came from.

*Summertime* (1894)

*Young Mother Sewing* (1900)

In France, Cassatt changed the way she painted, and took up a looser, fresher style. Her new paintings seem to brim with colour, as if lit by the afternoon sun streaming through a window. As subjects, she chose ordinary domestic scenes, often painting mothers with young children.

Unlike more conventional paintings, with formal poses and decorative costumes, Cassatt showed women dressed in the ordinary fashions of the day, holding infants who behaved like real children. *Maternal Caress,* for instance, shows a toddler seated on their mother's knee, reaching for her face. The pose perfectly captures the awkward movements of a small child.

*Maternal Caress* (1896)

Although Cassatt had broken with the conventions of art in her day, in later life, she had no time for new forms of art. When taken to see an exhibition of work by young artists – including Pablo Picasso and Paul Cezanne who would both go on to be world famous – she remarked, "I have never seen so many dreadful paintings in one place."

*Head of a Man*
by Pablo Picasso (1913)

*View of L'Estaque Through the Trees*
by Paul Cezanne (1879)

*Autumn, Portrait of Lydia Cassatt* (1880)

Sadly, Cassatt's own painting career came to an enforced end when she lost her sight in 1915. She died in 1926, at her home in France.

# 5 Edmonia Lewis (1844-1907)

Like Cassatt, Edmonia Lewis was an American artist who lived and worked in Europe. Both women were born in the same year, 1844, but their early life cannot have been more different. Lewis was the daughter of an African-American father and a Native-American mother,

Edmonia Lewis (c. 1870)

but both her parents had died by the time she was nine years old. She was then brought up by two aunts, who **eked** out a living selling souvenirs to tourists at Niagara Falls. As a child, Lewis was known by her Native-American name, Wildfire.

Lewis's life changed when her older brother made a fortune in the goldmines of California. He paid for her to go to a good school, and then to study art in Ohio. Inspired by public sculptures Lewis saw in the city, she decided to become a sculptor.

While she was an art student, Lewis met a number of wealthy **patrons** who supported her as she began her career.

Lewis's early work included portrait busts – a sculpture, just of the head and shoulders – of heroes from the anti-slavery movement and from the American **Civil War**, which was being fought at the time. She had a good head for business, producing plaster-cast copies of her bust of the war hero Colonel Shaw, which sold hundreds of copies. She made enough money to follow her dreams and move to Rome, in Italy.

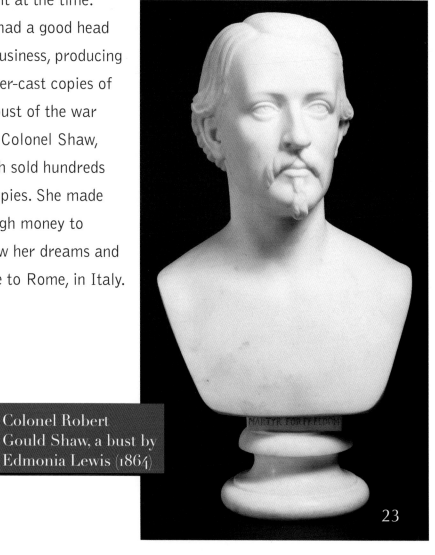

Colonel Robert Gould Shaw, a bust by Edmonia Lewis (1864)

MARTYR FOR FREEDOM

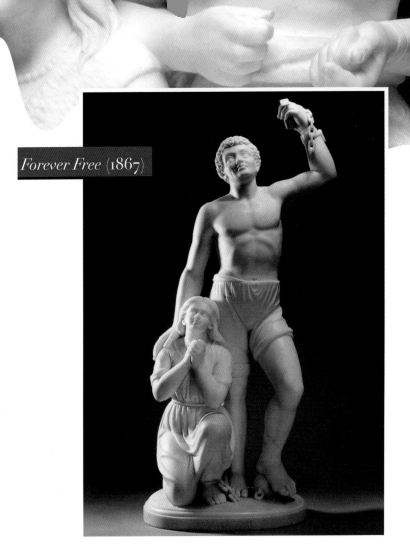

*Forever Free* (1867)

Being both a woman and a person of dual heritage, it was hard for Lewis to succeed as an artist in America at that time, without the support of her patrons. But in Rome it was possible for her to establish herself as a sculptor in her own right.

She chose to work in the Neo-Classical style, aiming to depict ideal versions of the human figure, inspired by the sculptures of ancient Greece and Rome.

She carved busts, figures and groups from blocks of white marble, and often chose subjects that reflected her own background, such as *Forever Free* which depicted a couple freed from slavery, and *Old Arrow Maker*, showing a Native-American family.

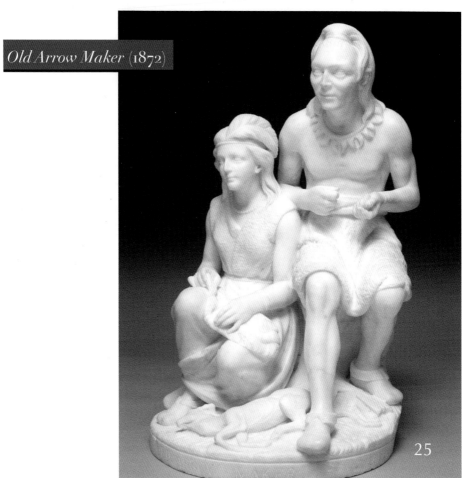

*Old Arrow Maker* (1872)

bust of Dr Dio Lewis (1968),
a prominent medic and
no relation to the artist

Little is known about Lewis's final years, other than that she moved to London, in England, where she died in 1907. For many years her grave was overgrown and forgotten, until in 2017, money was raised by an internet campaign and her final resting place was repaired and restored.

In some ways, Lewis may seem a strange choice for a book about rebel artists, because she chose to work in what was quite a conventional style. She didn't make art to challenge the establishment. She was even commissioned to make a portrait of the President of America. And yet, throughout her career, Lewis always worked in defiance of widespread prejudice. She was born at a time when many of her contemporaries lived as enslaved people. But she made art that called for a place at the heart of established society – that same society which so often viewed her as an inferior. Lewis made art that demanded equality.

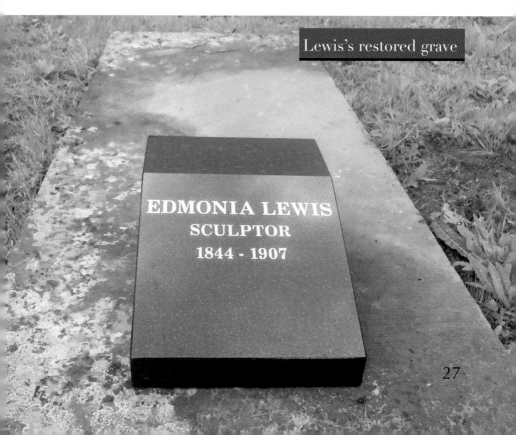

Lewis's restored grave

EDMONIA LEWIS
SCULPTOR
1844 - 1907

Georges Seurat was born in Paris in 1859, making him 15 years younger than Edmonia Lewis. But he only lived to be 31, so didn't get the chance to make as much art as he might have done had he lived longer. And yet the paintings he did produce, and the method he invented for making them, were

Georges Seurat (c. 1888)

like nothing that had come before, and would change the way many artists thought about their work.

As a young man, Seurat studied art in much the same way as every art student did in Europe at that time, by copying old paintings and making sketches and drawings of antique sculptures. But after he finished art school, Seurat decided to spend two years working only in black and white, learning all he could about how to depict light and shade. This was unusual.

In some ways, Seurat was as much a scientist as he was an artist. He was inspired by Impressionists like Mary Cassatt and the effects they created by painting very quickly, often in the open air. But Seurat wanted to make paintings with a more careful, thought-out approach. Unlike the Impressionists, Seurat would make sketches to try out his ideas before beginning a painting. And he didn't work outdoors, he painted in a studio, where he could take his time and have more control over his work.

*Trees* (study for *La Grande Jatte*) (1884)

Study for *A Sunday Afternoon on the Island of the Grande Jatte* (1884)

His painting *Sunday Afternoon on the Island of the Grande Jatte* measured three metres across and took two years to complete.

31

Seurat was just as fascinated by finding a way to depict the play of light and colour as the Impressionists were, but he invented his own method for doing this. He created his paintings by covering the surface of the canvas with thousands of tiny dots or flecks of colour.

Study for *The Channel at Gravelines, Evening* (1890)

But he didn't mix all the colours he needed first, as artists before him had usually done. Instead, if he wanted part of his painting to be green, say for a patch of grass by the side of a river, he would take some blue paint and some yellow paint and place tiny dots of each colour closely together.

Anyone looking at the whole painting would see a kind of mottled green, and yet close up, they could see each dot had its own colour. The yellow and the blue would blend together in the viewer's eye, to produce the effect of green. Seurat called this method "Pointillism", and he was among the first artists to use it in their work.

Seurat died of a sudden illness in 1891, leaving his final paintings unfinished. But in his short career, he'd found a new way of thinking about painting. Seurat saw colours the way a musician might think about notes.

*The Channel at Gravelines, Evening* (1890)

Playing several notes together creates different chords and sounds, and Seurat saw his tiny dots of colour in much the same way. He wanted to make art that was like music. As he himself once put it: "Art is harmony."

*The Eiffel Tower* (1889)

# 7 Hilma af Klint (1862-1944)

Seurat was among the first artists to use the Pointillist method in his work. But Hilma af Klint may have been the first artist ever to make an abstract painting. Abstract art became very popular from the 1950s onwards. But what is it?

af Klint in her studio (c. 1895)

An abstract painting might have colours and **tones**, shapes and angles, but it doesn't make a recognisable picture. A painting by Seurat, viewed up close, might seem to show nothing but dots of colour, but it's not abstract. It's a painting of something: an object, a person, or a landscape. A pattern or a design isn't abstract either, it's there simply to decorate a surface. Abstract painting isn't about decoration or showing things we see in the world around us. It's hard to say what it actually is, because every abstract artist might give a different answer. Some artists might be trying to express their emotions through the colours they choose, or the way they put the paint onto the canvas. Others might see abstract art as a way of describing a moment in time, or an idea, like the blueness of blue.

Af Klint may have been the first abstract artist inspired, in her case, by personal beliefs about the mystical nature of the universe. And yet almost nobody knew about her work until long after her death.

*The Swan, number 17* (1915)

Af Klint was born in 1862, the daughter of a captain in the Swedish Navy. As a child she was interested in mathematics and in botany, the study of plants. But she also showed artistic talent, and it was art she went on to study, at the Swedish Royal Academy. She became a painter of conventional landscapes, portraits and botanical drawings. These were skilfully done, but all quite ordinary. They were not the only art she produced, however. Over the years, she also made a large number of works she kept secret. They were abstract paintings.

*Late Summer* (1903), an example of the conventional style of painting af Klint exhibited to the public during her lifetime

Af Klint's attempts to interpret her mystical beliefs led her to make paintings that looked a little like complicated scientific diagrams, or objects seen under the lens of a powerful microscope. There were circles and triangles, and organic shapes, like parts of a plant. The shapes were often divided into brightly-coloured segments. Some were on large canvases, painted with oil paint, big enough to fill a gallery wall. Later, she switched to watercolours and worked on a smaller scale.

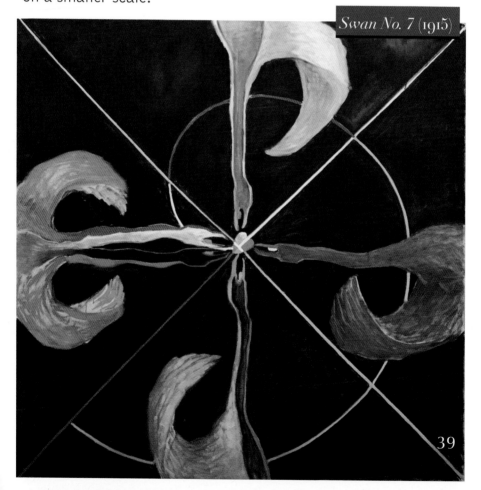

*Swan No. 7* (1915)

The paintings were not a total secret.
She did show some of them to a few friends.
But their unenthusiastic reaction led her to
think that the world was not ready for her
paintings, that they wouldn't be understood.
She kept all her abstracts hidden away in
a collection of wooden boxes. When she
died, she left the boxes to her nephew,
with instructions they should not be
opened until at least twenty years after
her death. When the boxes were finally
opened, in the late 1960s, nobody knew
what they'd find inside. By then, however,
abstract painting was a popular and
accepted form of modern art. Af Klint's
family were amazed to find that she'd been
producing abstracts many years before
anybody else. At last, the world was ready
for her paintings.

*The Dove, number 1* (1915)

# 8 Franz Marc (1880-1916)

Franz Marc (1910)

Franz Marc's father was
a professional landscape painter
working in a traditional style,
probably similar to the paintings
af Klint sold to make a living.
Franz Marc, however, would
grow up to become one of
the founders of German
Expressionism, a group of artists who wanted their work to
do more than record a pleasant view. With their bold use of
colour and line, the Expressionists wanted their art to show,
not just how the world looked, but also how they felt about it.

Born in Munich, in Germany, Marc studied art at the academy
in his home town, but later dropped out of classes and went
to live in Paris, France. Here he mixed with other artists
and began to form his own ideas. Marc came to believe that
**humanity** was losing touch with nature and the spiritual side
of life. He wanted to make art that challenged the world of
machines and cities.

Returning to Germany in 1911, he and a group of like-minded artist friends founded a journal, a kind of arts magazine. As well as producing the journal, the group also held exhibitions.

By now, Marc had developed a painting style of his own. His work usually featured animals. But he didn't want to make detailed, realistic drawings like Hokusai, or rapid, outdoor studies like the Impressionists. Marc's paintings combined abstract shapes with images of animals, not painted in their natural colours, but in blues, reds and yellows. To Marc, each colour, and each animal, had its own special meaning.

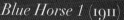
*Blue Horse 1* (1911)

*The Foxes* (1913)

*Fate of the Animals* (1913)

In 1913, Marc painted *Fate of the Animals*. This wasn't
like his other work, which usually showed animals in
peaceful scenes. Here, a great crowd of creatures seems to be
running away from an unseen enemy. A year later, the First
World War broke out and Marc was drafted into the army.
He wrote a letter home in which he said he thought his
painting *Fate of the Animals* had been like " ... a premonition
of this war – horrible and shattering".

The German authorities realised some of their best artists had
been sent to fight in the war. Eventually, they drew up a list,
and orders were given to transfer the artists home to safety.
Marc had come to be seen as an important artist, and his
name was on the list.

But sadly, the orders arrived too late. He had already lost his life at the Battle of Verdun, in 1916.

The battlefield at Verdun, France, 1916

45

# 9 Horace Pippin (1888-1946)

Marc's life was cut short, tragically, by the First World War. Horace Pippin was also sent to fight in the same conflict, with the US Army in 1918. Like Marc, Pippin hated the war, and he was badly wounded in the fighting. But he later said the experience

*Self-Portrait II* (1944)

"brought out all the art in me". It might be said that the war turned Pippin into an artist.

*The Getaway Fox* (1939)

In fact, it's more likely Pippin had always had the hand and eye of an artist. It was opportunity he lacked. Unlike the other artists in this book, Pippin didn't have any art training at all. He was entirely self-taught. But that didn't stop him producing art, when he finally got the chance.

Born in Pennsylvania, North America, and growing up an African-American child, in Goshen, New York State, Pippin showed early signs of artistic talent, drawing horses and jockeys at the racetrack near his home. But he had to leave school, aged 15, to get a job to help support his mother who had raised him single-handedly. After working as a hotel porter, a furniture packer and an iron moulder, Pippin enlisted in the army and was sent to fight in France. He was wounded in the right shoulder, and never fully regained the use of his arm.

*Sunday Morning Breakfast* (1943)

47

Recovering from this injury, back in America, Pippin began painting and drawing as part of his **physical therapy.** Once he started, he didn't stop. For the next 25 years, he painted. He painted scenes from his personal experience of the war, such as *Dog Fight over the Trenches.*

*Dog Fight over the Trenches* (1935)

He painted scenes from country life, and the history of
the anti-slavery movement in America, and work that
commented on the lives of African-Americans or highlighted
his concerns around racism.

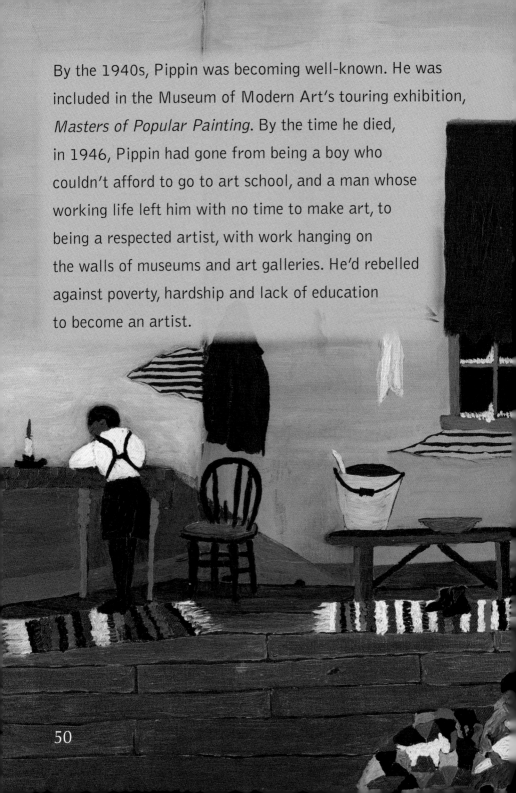

By the 1940s, Pippin was becoming well-known. He was included in the Museum of Modern Art's touring exhibition, *Masters of Popular Painting*. By the time he died, in 1946, Pippin had gone from being a boy who couldn't afford to go to art school, and a man whose working life left him with no time to make art, to being a respected artist, with work hanging on the walls of museums and art galleries. He'd rebelled against poverty, hardship and lack of education to become an artist.

*Interior* (1944)

# 10  Artists everywhere

In this book, we've looked at just a handful of artists, but there are many more out there, all with their own stories and different ways of working. Artists come from every part of the world, from every culture and period, from prehistoric times to the present day. Some aren't interested in breaking the rules, and instead, they work to become masters of a traditional style. A great many never have their names recorded, so we have no idea who they are. And yet their work is everywhere, in galleries and museums, or out on the streets. Art can be found far from the city, too, in forests and on hillsides, in jungles and deserts. Look around you, on the internet, in books and in magazines. Seek out the world's artists and learn to see with new eyes. You might want to see what kind of artist you could be, too, by studying art at school or university, or like Pippin, by teaching yourself to make art. There are all sorts of artists. Who knows? You, too, could be one of them.

# Glossary

canvas  fabric stretched on a frame, for painting on

civil war  a war between people of the same country

eked  to have made something (for example, money) last longer by using it sparingly

humanity  all human beings; can also mean kindness

patrons  people who help an artist's career, for instance by buying their work or paying their living expenses

physical therapy  treatment of injuries using methods such as exercise, massage, and so on, rather than medicines

still-life painting  a painting of an object or group of objects, often fruit or flowers

studio  an artist's workplace

tones  shades of light and dark

# Index

# What makes them rebel artists?

**Arcimboldo:** painted portraits assembled from objects

**Hokusai:** depicted a broad range of subjects; never stopped learning

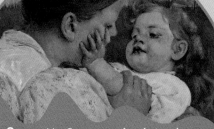

**Cassatt:** Impressionist who showed mothers and babies in a new light

**Seurat:** invented Pointillism

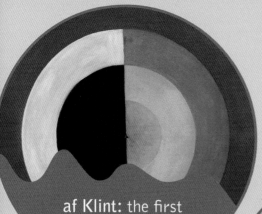

**af Klint:** the first abstract painter

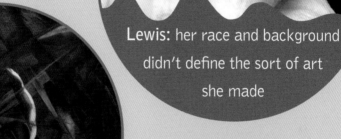

**Lewis:** her race and background didn't define the sort of art she made

**Marc:** used colour and form to explore his feelings about nature

**Pippin:** a self-taught artist

#  Ideas for reading

Written by Gill Matthews
*Primary Literacy Consultant*

**Reading objectives:**
- check that the book makes sense to them, discussing their understanding and exploring the meaning of words in context
- ask questions to improve their understanding
- retrieve, record and present information from non-fiction
- provide reasoned justifications for their views.

**Spoken language objectives:**
- articulate and justify answers, arguments and opinions
- use spoken language to develop understanding through speculating, hypothesising, imagining and exploring ideas
- participate in discussions, presentations, performances, role play, improvisations and debates

**Curriculum links:** Art – Great artists, architects and designers in history.

**Interest words:** culture, period, masters

**Resources:** IT, painting materials

## Build a context for reading

- Ask children to look closely at the image on the front cover. Discuss what they think they can see. Ask what the title means to them and discuss their understanding of the word 'rebel'.
- Read the back-cover blurb and explore what children think they will find out from the book. Explore which artists children are aware of and what they know about them.
- Ask what features they think this book might have. Give them time to skim through the book to find the contents, glossary and index. Discuss the purpose and organisation of each feature.

## Understand and apply reading strategies

- Ask children to turn to the contents list. Challenge them to work out how the book is organised.
- Ask them to turn to the Introduction together. Read pp2–3. Discuss children's reactions to what they have heard. Explore how they would describe an artist and what they do. How would they define a rebel artist?